VOLUME 57 OF THE YALE SERIES OF YOUNGER POETS, EDITED BY DUDLEY FITTS AND PUBLISHED WITH AID FROM THE MARY CADY TEW MEMORIAL FUND

CONTENTS

Series dedicated to young poets. It is as old as Granicus, and older. Neither is it an elaborately wrought poetry, though clearly there are moments when the anti-rhetoric becomes rhetorical in its own dissent. Others will find other pleasures or hesitations; I am moved chiefly by the plainness of Mr. Dugan's themes and by his nuances of imagery, phrasing, run, and rhythm. The cast of mind is hard, yet the detail is often wonderfully ingenuous and tender. There is a ferocious comic sense; but even while we are smiling over such a title as 'Cooled Heels Lament Against Frivolity, the 'Mask of Despair' we sense the urgently emotional counter-tendency at the beginning of that poem:

> Dugan's deathward, darling: you
> in your unseeable beauty, oh
> fictitious, legal person, need
> be only formally concerned . . .

To me that is a memorable cadence; and I have not heard anything quite like it. The beauty is certainly not unseeable, but I think that we must despair of fixing it by definition. Let us leave it, like Alexander's veteran, in the strange flood of art.

DUDLEY FITTS

it is something to be able to bring damp chaos under a modicum of control, to show a beginner that direct outpourings of emotion—no matter how 'strong', how 'alive', how 'beautiful'—are generally valid only for the sufferer at the moment, and it is only out of ordering that art springs. Little more is possible; and there is no Workshop this side of Heaven that can teach such writing as

> The wind came in for several thousand miles all night
> and changed the close lie of your hair this morning

where Mr. Dugan has combined the immense with the minute and released a magic that utters both; or, more intricately,

> These were the works,
> the prides and hat-trees of the head
> that climbed out of the brain
> to show its matter: earth, and how a beast
> who wears a potted plant, all thorns,
> is mostly desert, plus a glory
> unsustained

or the elegantly *un*fashionable daring that declares the 'moral', for all the world like a Burns or a Longfellow, in 'Funeral Oration for a Mouse':

> So,
> Lord, accept our felt though minor guilt
> for an ignoble foe and ancient sin:
> the murder of a guest
> who shared our board: just once he ate
> too slowly, dying in our trap
> from necessary hunger and a broken back.

These passages have the strangeness that I have mentioned without being able to define, and it is because of them, and of many others like them, that I take pleasure from Mr. Dugan's work.

This is not a young poetry, though it appears in a

Battle of Granicus
has just been won
by all of the Greeks except
the Lacedaemonians and
myself: this is a joke
between me and a man
named Alexander, whom
all of you ba-bas
will hear of as a god.'

That talk seems straight enough, in all conscience. Yet I have spoken of a queerness, a strangeness; and I am aware of an extraordinary tension, too, in spite of the greyness of diction and versification. Or, it may be, because of that greyness. This free-and-easy survivor, this least *gloriosus* of veterans, has rejected the splendors of history that ba-bas record for other ba-bas to read, and has achieved ('and/myself') an individual, anti-heroic, apart-from-the-mob victory that seems to dwarf Alexander's. He alone has done it, or he and the missing Spartans, and it is a victory worth winning in an age of togetherness. But though this may be the import of the poem, as I take it to be, it is not in itself the poem or the reason for the poem. Nor is the artful flatness of speech—the drained quality, the stultification of all that tradition leads us to expect in battle pieces, particularly in battle pieces *all' antico*—the essence of the poem; although we may say that this quality, being a matter of tone, is something that the fashionable new criticism might profitably investigate as a 'strategy'. Everything fails us, ultimately, in our attempt to account for what the poem does for us. 'This is strange,' we say, 'but I—' 'Therefore' would be more just than 'but'. The strangeness is the poem.

Writing can not be taught, because strangeness can not be taught. Least of all can one be taught how to be a poet. Technical decorum (or the necessary indecorum) can be communicated, up to a certain point, and there is a pretty apparatus of tricks and gambols that the leaders of Poetry Workshops can pass on to their corybants; but there is no formula to make a poet out of a verser or worse. Of course

FOREWORD

We begin with facts. On 22 May 334 B.C., Alexander the Great defeated the Persians at the river Granicus, and from there he went on to conquer the rest of Asia Minor. Granicus was a famous victory, with Alexander's thirty thousand routing the six hundred thousand of Darius; and we have the inscription composed by Alexander himself in which he remarks that he won the battle 'with no help from the Lacedaemonians'. Generals are not normally so petulant in their moments of self-congratulation, and inscriptions by their nature entail being economical with words; hence our fancy is struck by those absent Spartans, who seem indeed, though in a negative way, to matter almost more than the combatants themselves. Where were the Lacedaemonians? Were they combing their long hair? Were they at home in bed on this antique Feast of Crispin Crispian? So history, even in this obscure record, teases the mind; but I cite it here because it has teased Mr. Dugan's specifically, and because it has somehow resulted in 'How We Heard the Name', a poem that delights me.

I wish that I could account entirely for that delight. History is not really helpful. Alexander is a fact, Granicus is a fact, even the Spartans are what Mr. E. E. Cummings might call an unfact; but they are only the material that has passed into an aesthetic and philosophical fact that seems queerly remote from its origin. A strangeness surrounds the soldier who comes floating down that Bithynian river:

> He seemed drunk
> and we asked him Why
> had he and this junk
> come down to us so
> from the past upstream.
> 'Friends,' he said, 'the great

FOR JUDY

Acknowledgment is made to the following magazines for poems originally appearing in them:

Poetry (Chicago): Prison Song; Oasis; The Natural Enemies of the Conch; Imperial Song for Warmth; The Branches of Water or Desire; Portrait ("The captive flourished like"); Landfall; Notes Toward a Spring Offensive; Actual Vision of Morning's Extrusion; How We Heard the Name; On an East Wind from the Wars; Philodendron.

Accent: Love Song: I and Thou; On Hurricane Jackson; Poem ("The person who can do").

The New Yorker: The Stutterer.

The poem now entitled "Sixteen Lines on Marching" was published in *Cross-Section 1947,* ed. Edwin Seaver; permission to reprint it is gratefully acknowledged.

POEMS

BY ALAN DUGAN

Foreword by Dudley Fitts

NEW HAVEN: YALE UNIVERSITY PRESS, 1961

This Morning Here

This is this morning: all
the evils and glories of last night
are gone except for their
effects: the great world wars
I and II, the great marriage
of Edward the VII or VIII
to Wallis Warfield Simpson and
the rockets numbered like the Popes
have incandesced in flight
or broken on the moon: now
the new day with its famous
beauties to be seized at once
has started and the clerks
have swept the sidewalks
to the curb, the glass doors
are open, and the first
customers walk up and down
the supermarket alleys of their eyes
to Muzak. Every item has
been cut out of its nature,
wrapped disguised as something
else, and sold clean by fractions.
Who can multiply and conquer
by the Roman numbers? Lacking
the Arab frenzy of the zero, they
have obsolesced: the butchers
have washed up and left
after having killed and dressed
the bodies of the lambs all night,
and those who never have seen blood awake
can drink it browned
and call the past an unrepeatable mistake
because this circus of their present is all gravy.

On an East Wind from the Wars

The wind came in for several thousand miles all night
and changed the close lie of your hair this morning. It
has brought well-travelled sea-birds who forget
their passage, singing. Old songs from the old
battle- and burial-grounds seem new in new lands.
They have to do with spring as new in seeming as
the old air idling in your hair in fact. So new,
so ignorant of any weather not your own,
you like it, breathing in a wind that swept
the battlefields of their worst smells, and took the dead
unburied to the potter's field of air. For miles
they sweetened on the sea-spray, the foul washed off,
and what is left is spring to you, love, sweet,
the salt blown past your shoulder luckily. No
wonder your laugh rings like a chisel as it cuts
your children's new names in the tombstone of thin air.

On an Old Advertisement and After a Photograph by Alfred Stieglitz

The formal, blooded stallion, the Arabian,
will stand for stud at fifty bucks a throw,
but there is naturally a richer commerce in his act,
eased in this instance by a human palm
and greased with money: the quiver in his haunch
is not from flies, no; the hollow-sounding,
kitten-crushing hooves are sharp and blind,
the hind ones hunting purchase while the fore
rake at the mare's flank of the sky.
Also, the two- or three-foot prick that curls
the mare's lip back in solar ecstasy
is greater than the sum of its desiring:
the great helm of the glans, the head
of feeling in the dark, is what spits out,
beyond itself, its rankly generative cream.
After that heat, the scraggled, stallion-legged foal
is not as foolish as his acts: the bucking and
the splayed-out forelegs while at grass
are practices: he runs along her flank
in felt emergencies, inspired by love to be
his own sweet profit of the fee and the desire,
compounded at more interest than the fifty in the bank.

Philodendron

The person of this plant with heart-shaped leaves
and off-shot stalks, bending at each knee,
is built of dishwater, cigarette smoke, no
sunlight, and humus mixed with peat-moss. Like
genius, it survives our inattention and the dark,
potted like myself indoors, and goes on growing.
It grows for no known cause that I can find
outside itself, by means of mumbling, flowering
no flowers, no flowers, none for all these years.

*Balance and survival: it has
a strategy of elbows as
it breaks its hairy knees
while climbing up the wall
and then juts off again,
shaped like a claw.*

Since imagination has the answer to these noes,
imagine it as one of those survivors in the old
swamps, shadowed by the grown, light-headed conifers:
fit for the damps, whose gentlest odor seems
corrosive, mightily akin to older, shadowed ferns,
it might have dropped its pollen in the black
water where the pollen swam, and thus become
perseverant in going on in lust, like us,
and mobile through its young. Even now

*Even at its top most
broken elbow, it
must turn uprooted from
its heaven in the air,
and, in going down,
not find it on the floor,*

it does move on in time, too, each elbow putting out
a stalk and leaf in faith and doubt, but no
flowers. Who knows what in hell it loves or lacks
as crawler in arrest. Sometimes to water it,
to notice it, to keep it out of the bureau drawer
and trained to climb perennially around itself,
is piety enough toward indoor plants right now
when one is thirsty, too, for rich lost tastes
and light streaming down through amniotic air.

*either. Compelled to move
anyhow, it always has
an angle and an out
in going nowhere, all
around itself
in faith and doubt.*

Imperial Song for Warmth

Snow that makes graces on a soldier's sleeve
is ordered rain, the crystal wheels
each agony is strapped to in his business:
waiting in the lee of enemies.
The rain that duplicates forever
can make news again,
distinction in each flake,
but snow is not his order, ordering.

The lesser orders, like the ants,
the spiders, and platoons of snow,
make wholes by ruined parts:
frozen in wait, or jungled monkey-wise,
they organize by jeopardies,
atrocious in design.
Oh web, geometry of appetite,
oh darkly ordered, muted ants,
the snow is not in order, ordering.

Fire and ice burn unalike:
the flakes have touches for his skin,
his eyebrows, and the hair
his hand is aped with; what
exasperation of survival that the snow,
with careful walking,
cracks like salt in the boot
or infiltrates more loving warmth.
Baled in rags
and like a haystack, warm at heart,
unhurt he is a center of decay,

but once the heat is hurt,
the snow for lashes, dusted on his eyes,
will fill his wrinkles of fatigue

with tracery, will cover him to death
with tracery, a thread of shuttles
webbed to net a death. Oh air,
diamond of ice,
the wound is mammoth, fixed in glacial ice:
its trivial grimace will bloom
as rotten ice at thaw.

So which is better, to campaign
between the Tropics where
immediate bulbs of sweat
flower in stains on his fatigues
and rot the living, or among
geodesic spiders of ice?
The latter children nest in a grotesque,
but southward, with the butcher ants,
the death does not
go uniformed in flesh all winter long,
far from the monkey's eulogy,
nor do the wheels of snow
bunch in the lee of his crystal ear
and hum the umbra's note:
Earth makes night, snow is black
in ordering his brain to stop.

6

Prison Song

The skin ripples over my body like moon-wooed water,
rearing to escape me. Where would it find another
animal as naked as this one it hates to cover?
Once it told me what was happening outside,
who was attacking, who caressing, and what the air
was doing to feed or freeze me. Now I wake up
dark at night, in a textureless ocean of ignorance,
or fruit bites back and water bruises like a stone:
a jealousy, because I look for other tools to know
with, and another armor, better fitted to my flesh.
So, let it lie, turn off its clues, or try to leave:
sewn on me seamless like those painful shirts
the body-hating saints wore, this sheath of hell
is pierced to my darkness nonetheless: what traitors
labor in my face, what hints they smuggle through
its itching guard! But even in the night it jails,
with nothing but its lies and silences to feed upon,
the jail itself can make a scenery, sing prison songs
and set off fireworks to praise a homemade day.

The So-called Wild Horses of the Water

The so-called wild horses of the water
stumbled all over the boulders
and fell steaming and foaming over
the world's edge down the roaring
white way of the waterfall
into the black pool of the death
of motion at the bottom where
the cold stoned water lay
dense as a diamond of pressure and
the eye of silence stared unmoved
at the world's cavalry falling in
to be the seer not the heard again.

Landfall

The curtains belly in the waking room.
Sails are round with holding, horned at top,
and net a blue bull in the wind: the day.
They drag the blunt hulls of my heels awake
and outrigged by myself through morning seas.
If I do land, let breakfast harbor me.

Waking in June, I found a first fruit
riding out the water on a broken branch.
Sleep was a windfall, and its floating seeds
steered me among the Cyclades of noise.
A coastal woman with a cricket in her hair
took soundings as the time chirped in her head:
I knew that night-time is an Island District;
curtains are my sails to shore.

Block and tackle string a butcher's dance
to hoist the sun on home: the bull
is beached and hung to dry, and through
his bloody noon, the island of his flank
quakes in the silence and disturbs the flies.

Flesh has crawled out on the beach of morning,
salt-eyed, with the ocean wild in hair,
and landed, land-locked, beached on day,
must hitch its hand to traces and resist
the fierce domestic horses teamed to it.

Drivers and driven both, the plowing heels
bloody the furrows after plunging beasts:
the spring of day is fleshed for winter fruit.
Fallen in salt-sweat, piercing skin, the bones
essay plantation in their dirt of home

and rest their aching portion in the heat's
blood afternoon. O if the sun's day-laborer
records inheritable yield, the script
is morning's alpha to omega after dark:
the figured head to scrotum of the bull.

Accountancy at sundown is the wine of night:
walking the shore, I am refreshed by it
and price the windrise and the bellowing surf
while, waiting for its freight of oil and hides,
a first sail starts the wind by snapping whips.

Sixteen Lines on Marching

In spring when the ego arose from the genitals
after a winter's refrigeration, the sergeants
were angry: it was a time of looking
to the right and left instead of straight ahead.

Now the rich lost tastes have been lost again,
the green girls grown brown for another year:
intelligent bodies make ready for the entropy begun
by north winds and the declination of the sun.

Say death, soldiering, or fear: these words
are luxuries no more but the true words of winter
when the flesh hardens and collects itself around
the skeleton to protect what little it contains.

If anything is to happen let it happen now.
If anything is expected of us let the orders be cut
immediately and read Winter; the proper season
for caution. Match, if you can, its coldness: spring.

Love Song: I and Thou

Nothing is plumb, level or square:
   the studs are bowed, the joists
are shaky by nature, no piece fits
   any other piece without a gap
or pinch, and bent nails
   dance all over the surfacing
like maggots. By Christ
   I am no carpenter. I built
the roof for myself, the walls
   for myself, the floors
for myself, and got
   hung up in it myself. I
danced with a purple thumb
   at this house-warming, drunk
with my prime whiskey: rage.
   Oh I spat rage's nails
into the frame-up of my work:
   it held. It settled plumb,
level, solid, square and true
   for that great moment. Then
it screamed and went on through,
   skewing as wrong the other way.
God damned it. This is hell,
   but I planned it, I sawed it,
I nailed it, and I
   will live in it until it kills me.
I can nail my left palm
   to the left-hand cross-piece but
I can't do everything myself.
   I need a hand to nail the right,
a help, a love, a you, a wife.

The Natural Enemies of the Conch

1

The first point of the shell
was moored to zero but
its mouth kissed one
and paid in torque.
A turbine in the conch
is whirled so fast
that it stands still,
humming with cold light.

2

The animal inside
is out of luck in art.
Tourists gouge him out
of water's Gabriel
and gild the whirling horn
to make a lamp of home.
The death, a minor surf,
sounds in the living room.

3

(That's the way it is
with the ugly: ugliness
should arm their flesh
against the greedy but
they grow such wiles
around the hurt
that estheticians come
with love, apology

13

and knives and cut
the beauty from the quick.)

4

The Maya crack the gem
where muscles glue
the palace to the slug
and eat him out. Again
the curio is fleshed
but wrecked like Knossos
with a window down the maze
toward nothing
where a bull at heart
roars in the start of surf.

5

(To know why slime
should build such forts,
challenge the tooth
one pod is spurred with.
He has a tongue on guard,
like authors, out around
the works, and can retreat
in what reveals him,
claw last, at a touch.)

6

Turned in his likeness
like a foraging son,
there is a Natural Drill
that bores a vent in him
and taps his life.

Like Prince Hippolytus,
when we behave too
simply toward some law
we have our image,
father, from the sea:
the sea-bull bellowing
to foul our traces,
dragging us to death
behind disturbed machines.

7

The snail retreats to nothing
where the shell is born,
pearl of its phlegm and rock,
small as water can whirl.
Whorling down the turns
from mouth to point,
it points in vanishing
to university,
where thickened water learned
one graph with nebulae
and turned the living horn
on zero's variable lathe.

8

It voids the plum, wrack
and accidents of space
and sounds a sea-bull
first ashore. Similar ears,
listening mouth to mouth,
hear it as ocean's time
and turn into the brain
as mirrors of the maze.

Importation of Landscapes

The seed of an iron flower
must grow in gravel
or else make its own
if it is taken from the desert
and sunk in loam.
What a hard garden,
lovers: iron is used
to the routine of oil
but gets the bloody rust
in damp: there, the oasis,
a devotion in the sand,
prays flesh, virus to mammoth,
and supports them all,
but when the regular iron
flowers in sensuous ease
it languishes; the bloom
weeps dust. Spear-shaped,
venomous as plows were thought to be,
the leaves fall sick
and make a desert: iron's
oasis in delight
and field of strength.

Portrait

The captive flourished like
a mushroom in his oubliette.
He breathed his night's breath every day,
took food and water from the walls
and ruled his noisy rats and youth.
He made a calendar of darkness,
thought his boredom out, and carved
Heaven in his dungeon with a broken spoon.

At last he made his own
light like a deep sea fish, and when
his captors' children came for him
they found no madman in a filthy beard
or heap of rat-picked bones:
they found a spry, pale old gentleman
who had a light around his head.
Oh he could stare as well as ever,
argue in a passionate voice
and walk on to the next
detention in their stone dismay
unaided.

Oasis

Whelped from blackness by a pressure of rocks,
black water rose like breath from the lungs
and burst in speech. It poured its glitter,
trouble, on the sand, and babbled on about
its quick exploits in shape above the plain.
This speaking taught the desert thirst: once
sucked-at by that thirster, sand, the water spread
its cool hair over fever: sand was changed:
what was almost sand in sand, the waiting sand,
a hidden seed, leaped up and burst in palms!
The water argued greenery to sand: now sand
is passionate with fruit! Ticking with bugs,
bustling with flowers and death, the garden is
a place and fireworks, a green wild on the calm.

Oh its mirages offer water, figs, and shade
to windrift birds for songs and wings of praise.
Clock-lost nomads, lost in the running sands,
will have to choose, when madness lights
advertisements of water to their soaking need,
if they will drop to the truth of desert, dry
to sand, or run to where the fanfare of quick
water winds their clocks, gives place to love,
and lets them drink their living from its deaths.

What Happened? What Do You Expect?

The waiter waited, the cook ate,
the scales read zero, and the clock
began to agree. It agreed
and disagreed but rang no bells,
and in the quiet of the whole
peeled onion on the chopping block
the whole flayed lamb stamped
                QUALITY
hung by its heels and was
devoured by a fly. Outside,
a woman screamed and stopped.
Two cops came in for coffee-and,
laughing and filling the place
with night as black as the sweat
in the armpits of their shirts.
"Some guy hit his girl friend
and she didn't like it or us
either." Oh it had been
the count-down for a great
catastrophe that had not
happened, not as raw event,
but as time in the death of the lamb.

On Hurricane Jackson

Now his nose's bridge is broken, one eye
will not focus and the other is a stray;
trainers whisper in his mouth while one ear
listens to itself, clenched like a fist;
generally shadow-boxing in a smoky room,
his mind hides like the aching boys
who lost a contest in the Pan-Hellenic games
and had to take the back roads home,
but someone else, his perfect youth,
laureled in newsprint and dollar bills,
triumphs forever on the great white way
to the statistical Sparta of the champs.

Poem

The person who can do
accounts receivable as fast
as steel machines and out-
talk telephones, has wiped
her business lipstick off,
undone her girdle and belts
and stepped down sighing from
the black quoins of her heels
to be the quiet smiler with
changed eyes. After long-
haired women have unwired
their pencil-pierced buns, it's an
event with pennants when
the Great Falls of emotion say
that beauty is in residence,
grand in her hotel of flesh,
and Venus of the marriage manual,
haloed by a diaphragm,
steps from the shell *Mercenaria*
to her constitutional majesty
in the red world of love.

The Branches of Water or Desire

Imagine that the fast life of a bird
sang in the branches of the cold
cast-off antlers of a stag
and lit the points of bone
with noises like St. Elmo's fire.
Worn, those antlers were
an outer counterweight,
extravagant in air and poised
against a branching need
drumming in the red inside
the arteries or antlers of the heart.
That was the balance that allowed
the stag's head's limber rise,
and might have been the gift
the temporary, reed-boned bird
sang air about: abundance,
rank beyond the need. The horns
appear before the eye to be
more permanent than songs
that branch out lightly on the air
or root into the chest
as singing's negative, the breath,
that touches at the branching veins
at depth:
but when the leaping rut
slept growing in the hollow of the hind,
the candelabra that the head
dazzled the wedding with
guttered to rubbish and were cast.
That perch for calls and bird-
song was a call itself,
and fell to grace the wilds
correctly, since an itch,
under the rootholds of the horns,

whitens with mushroom wants
in cellars of the antlers' nerves
just off the brain,
and wants to make its many points again.

Once cast, they are the dead and fall
duly as a sound falls in the cool
of smoking days, when air
sags with the damp and song
swirls in the hollows: this
is so the works can start again,
untrammeled by the done, downed
wonders, and be upstart news
to publicize the crocus of next spring.
The stag had something on his mind
beside his wants, and it
is more than curious, the way
the horns are worn at ease
by cranial fulcrums, since the like of them,
the lighter songs or battle-cries of birds,
hum in the chambers of the nose
just off the brain,
so that the chambered mute, the brain,
silent in wants and plans,
vibrates in closest sympathy
with what is not its own
and plays as best it can.

Those were the works,
the prides and hat-trees of the head
that climbed out of the brain
to show its matter: earth, and how a beast
who wears a potted plant, all thorns,
is mostly desert, plus a glory
unsustained. Oh it
is useless in a fight
won by the head and heels,
not nicety, not war-cries worn

in silence to be seen. The hinds,
cropping the perimeter of war,
sooner accept the runnel one
who has not fronded his desire
with public works. Call and be gone,
bird: the one who wears the horns
can bear the singer too, mindlessly singing all
the bird-brained airs of spring,
but has to cast the tuning forks
that let the eye see song,
and winter with this loss.

The bone as singing-post
is capital enough in arms
to hold the nation of your sound
in singing's fief: the brain's
savage receptionist, the ear,
beating a drum outside its closest door,
joins with the civil eye's
electrical distance from the brain
in witnessing the poles of prongs and sounds
arcing across their earthworks of desire:

the sounds and tines
must be some excess of the flesh
that wants beyond efficiency
in time, but cannot find
much permanence outside it: getting or not aside,
it must branch out in works
that cap itself, for some
imaginary reason out of mind.

Memorial Service for the Invasion Beach
Where the Vacation in the Flesh Is Over

I see that there it is on the beach. It is
ahead of me and I walk toward it: its
following vultures and contemptible dogs
are with it, and I walk toward it. If,
in the approach to it, I turn my back
to it, then I walk backwards: I
approach it as a limit. Even if I fall
to hands and knees, I crawl to it.
Backwards or forwards I approach it.

There is the land on one hand, rising, and
the ocean on the other, falling away;
what the sky does, I can not look to see,
but it's around, as ever, all around.
The courteous vultures move away in groups
like functionaries. The dogs circle and stare
like working police. One wants a heel
and gets it. I approach it, concentrating so
on not approaching it, going so far away
that when I get there I am sideways like
the crab, too limited by carapace to say:

"Oh here I am arrived, all; yours today."
No: kneeling and facing away, I will
fall over backwards in intensity of life
and lie convulsed, downed struggling,
sideways even, and should a vulture ask
an eye as its aperitif, I grant it,
glad for the moment wrestling by a horse
whose belly has been hollowed from the rear,
who's eyeless. The wild dog trapped in its ribs
grins as it eats its way to freedom. Not
conquered outwardly, and after rising once,
I fall away inside, and see the sky around
rush out away into the vulture's craw
and barely can not hear them calling, "Here's one."

Portrait

He wore the burnt-cork moustache and coonskin cap
that all the other boy pirate captains wore
in the comic strips, and when he smiled, real
Douglas Fairbanks diamonds glittered in his eyes
and teeth, but the first mate knew that he
was worried about his father: the fine old
gentleman, chuckling, firm, but kind,
had not been seen for several episodes.
Then it became clear: behind his smiles
and flashing gallantry there were two
serious drives: 1. Concern for the lost father,
and: 2. Worship of fuel as a god,
whether of gas or air, to drive or sail
him forward, always forward in the search,
although the old man had been dropped astern.

Mockery Against the Irish Censorship

Ireland was better in its dream,
with the oppressor foreign.
Now its art leaves home to keen
and its voice is orange.
It is a sad revolt, for loving's health,
that beats its enemy and then itself.

Now that Irishmen are free
to enslave themselves together
they say that it is better they
do worst to one another
than have the english do them good
in an exchange of joy for blood.

A just as alien pius blacks
their greens of lovers' commerce;
rehearsing victory, they lack
a government to fill its promise.
Worse, law has slacked the silly harp
that was their once and only Ark

out, and I am sorry to be flip
and narrowly disrespectful,
but since I wade at home in it
I stoop and take a mouthful
to splatter the thick walls of their heads
with American insult! Irish sense is dead.

Weeds as Partial Survivors

The chorus of the weeds, unnameably
profuse, sings Courage, Courage, like
an India of unemployables who have
no other word to say and say it.
Too bendable to break, bowing away
together from the wind although
the hail or hurricane can knock them flat,
they rise up wet by morning. This
morning erection of the weeds
is not so funny: It
is perseverance dancing: some of them,
the worst, are barely rooted and
a lady gardener can pull them out
ungloved. Nevertheless, they do do
what they do or die, surviving all
catastrophes except the human: they
extend their glosses, like the words I said,
on sun-cracked margins of the sown
lines of our harrowed grains.

The Mirror Perilous

I guess there is a garden named
"Garden of Love." If so, I'm in it:
I am the guesser in the garden.
There is a notice by the central pond
that reads: "Property of Narcissus.
Trespass at your own risk,"
so I went there. That is where,
having won but disdained a lady,
he fell for his own face and died,
rightly, "not having followed through,"
as the sentence read, read by the lady:
Oh you could hear her crying all about
the wilderness and wickedness of law.
I looked in that famous mirror perilous
and it wasn't much: my own face,
beautiful, and at the bottom,
bone, a rusty knife, two beads,
and something else I cannot name.
I drank my own lips on the dare
but could not drink the lips away.
The water was heavy, cool, and clear,
but did not quench. A lady laughed
behind my back; I learned the worst:
I could take it or leave it, go or stay,
and went back to the office drunk,
possessed of an echo but not a fate.

Letter to Eve

The lion and lioness are intractable,
the leaves are covered with dust,
and even the peacocks will not
preen. You should come back,
burnish us with your former look,
and let the search for truth
go. After a loud sleep last night
I got up late and saw a new
expression on the faces of the deer;
the shrews and wolves are gaunt
and out of sorts: they nosed
their usual fruits and do not know
what they intend to do. The dogs
got tangled up in an unusual way:
one put its urinary tube
into the other's urinary tract
and could not get it out.
Standing tail to tail for hours,
they looked at me with wise,
supplicatory eyes. I named
two new sounds: snarl and shriek,
and hitherto unnoticed bells,
which used to perform the air,
exploded!, making a difference.
Come back before the garden does
what I'll call "die," not that it
matters. Rib, Rib, I have a new
opinion of your Eve, called "lust"
or Love, I don't know which,
and want to know how I will choose.

31

Against France: On the Algerian
Pleasures of Entity

When I died the devils tortured me with icepicks and pliers
and all the other instruments they learned from men of faith;
they took off my genitals and nails, less troubles, chained me
to the wall, and came in shifts with forced foods and elec-
     trodes.

Later, after works, I tore the chains from the wall. What whips
chains are! I lashed my lashers and escaped their cell,
armed to my last two teeth in search of god. My arms, though,
were chains chained to my arms, so what I touched I struck.

I met all the animals with beaks and offered them myself
to rend, since, as a student of torture, I had found it fun,
and wrecked them as they bit. What would I have done
if I had met a smile? Well, I swam the river of spit,

crossed a plain of scorpions, and went into the lake
of fire. I emerged bone, dripping the last of my flesh,
a good riddance, and asked whoever came to chew the bones,
"Where is god?" Each answered: "Here I am, now. I am,

in a way." I answered, "Nonsense!" every time and struck
with chains. Weary, weary, I came to the final ocean of acid:
pain was a friend who told me I was temporal when nothing
else spoke, so I dipped in my hand-bones and saw them eaten.

"It is good to be rid of the bones," I felt, "as clattering
encumbrances to search," and dived in whole. However,
instead of being shriven or freed up into flight, oh I
was born again. I squalled for a while to keep my death,

that time when chains were arms and pain a great ally,
but I was conquered and began my sentence to a child's
forgetfulness, uneager to collect the matter of these dreams,
and stared into the present of you innocent beasts.

Funeral Oration for a Mouse

This, Lord, was an anxious brother and
a living diagram of fear: full of health himself,
      he brought diseases like a gift
to give his hosts. Masked in a cat's moustache
but sounding like a bird, he was a ghost
      of lesser noises and a kitchen pest
for whom some ladies stand on chairs. So,
Lord, accept our felt though minor guilt
      for an ignoble foe and ancient sin:
            the murder of a guest
who shared our board: just once he ate
      too slowly, dying in our trap
from necessary hunger and a broken back.

Humors of love aside, the mousetrap was our own
opinion of the mouse, but for the mouse
      it was the tree of knowledge with
its consequential fruit, the true cross
and the gate of hell. Even to approach
      it makes him like or better than
its maker: his courage as a spoiler never once
impressed us, but to go out cautiously at night,
into the dining room;—what bravery, what
      hunger! Younger by far, in dying he
was older than us all: his mobile tail and nose
spasmed in the pinch of our annoyance. Why,
then, at that snapping sound, did we, victorious,
      begin to laugh without delight?

Our stomachs, deep in an analysis
      of their own stolen baits
(and asking, "Lord, Host, to whom are we the pests?"),
      contracted and demanded a retreat
from our machine and its effect of death,

33

as if the mouse's fingers, skinnier
than hairpins and as breakable as cheese,
could grasp our grasping lives, and in
their drowning movement pull us under too,
into the common death beyond the mousetrap.

I. Enigma: Calm: Addressed to the Air

There is the grass to play
with, standing as stiff as nails.

A piece of paper which
was rattled for a week
limps in the lounging air.

Even this breath, all wind
down to the purple lungs
can not blow up a breeze
to clear us out of here.

II. Comment on I.

Here there are armored snails
climbing the grass-blades single file.
Certain as iron-clads and as dumb,
they try the heights between
the razor edges of the salt grass
and come a cropper: up
there at the grasses' tips,
swaying in windlessness,
they have to fall. What
will happen to us all
while smothered by the air's
inaction? Slow ourselves,
and waiting for a wind to rise,
we must expect disaster, but
the air is not a savior, iron not
a damned good armor for a fool,
though even love becomes
a doldrum in the tidal
salt-flats of what's beautiful.

How We Heard the Name

The river brought down
dead horses, dead men
and military debris,
indicative of war
or official acts upstream,
but it went by, it all
goes by, that is the thing
about the river. Then
a soldier on a log
went by. He seemed drunk
and we asked him Why
had he and this junk
come down to us so
from the past upstream.
"Friends," he said, "the great
Battle of Granicus
has just been won
by all of the Greeks except
the Lacedaemonians and
myself: this is a joke
between me and a man
named Alexander, whom
all of you ba-bas
will hear of as a god."

Morning Song

Look, it's morning, and a little water gurgles in the tap.
I wake up waiting, because it's Sunday, and turn twice more
than usual in bed, before I rise to cereal and comic strips.
I have risen to the morning danger and feel proud,
and after shaving off the night's disguises, after searching
close to the bone for blood, and finding only a little,
I shall walk out bravely into the daily accident.

Orpheus

Singing, always singing, he was something
of a prig, like Rilke, and as dangerous
to women. They butchered him; but loud
as ever, wanted or not, the bloody head
continued singing as it drifted out to sea.

Always telling, brave in counsel, ruthlessly glib,
he tamed that barbarous drunk, Dionysus,
out of his ecstasy, and taught the Greeks,
once dirt to the gods and damned to hell,
to pray for heaven, godhood, and himself.

O Maenads, who could choke off his revolt?
Shrined as an oracle, the lovely head
went on with its talking, talking, talking,
until the god, the jealous Apollo himself,
came down in a rage and shut it off.

Tribute to Kafka for Someone Taken

The party is going strong.
The doorbell rings. It's
for someone named me.
I'm coming. I take
a last drink, a last
puff on a cigarette,
a last kiss at a girl,
and step into the hall,
                          bang,
shutting out the laughter. "Is
your name you?" "Yes."
"Well come along then."
"See here. See here. See here."

Notes Toward a Spring Offensive

I will begin again in May, describing weather, how
the wind swept up the dust and pigeons suddenly. Then
the rain began to fall on this and that, the regular
ablutions. The soldiers marched, the cowards wept,
and all were wetted down and winded, crushed.
Soldiers turn the dew to mud. Shivering uncontrollably
because the mild wind blew through wet fatigues,
they fell down in the mud, their pieces fouled,
and groveled in the wilderness, regardless. Some died, and
how
I will not tell, since I should speak of weather. Afterwards
the clouds were stripped out of the sky. Palpably fresh,
suckingly sweet like bitten peaches, sparkling like oh,
a peeling tangerine, the air was warmed by light again,
and those who could rise rose like crushed chives from the
mud
and stank and thought to dry. The cowards wept
and some got well again, profane with flowers, all was well,
and I have finished now in May. I have described
one circle of a day and those beneath it, but not why.

Transcribed Conversation in Praise of Cows

While it is so that you
can eat a pig from nose
to ass-hole and beyond,
the cow is usefuller:
the beef, beefsteak, broth,
are healthy, and the milk,
the fine glue from the hooves,
the leather and the horns,
Oh you can take one horn
and blow it and call up
whole armies of believers!

Actual Vision of Morning's Extrusion

Grey smoke rose from the morning ground
and separated into spheres. The smoke
or fog of each sphere coiled upon itself
like snakes at love, and hardened into brains:
the corals in the ocean of first light.
These brains grew shells. Mother of pearl, out
clattered the bones! Two ivies intertwined
ran down them searchingly, the red and white
of arteries and nerves, and found their ends.
Nerves hummed in the wind: the running blood,
in pulsing out a heart, induced a warm,
red haze of flesh around a hollow tube,
writhing with appetite, ejection, love,
and hardened in the temperature of dawn.
"Done!" said the clocks, and gave alarm.
Eyes popped into heads as tears amazed.
All hair stood out. All moved and rose
and took a breath: two gasping voids
turned blue with it around the heart.
Shocked into teeth and nails and wrapped
in winding sheets of skin, all souls walked
to test their creatures in their joints,
chinks, and armors as the walking dead,
curious as to what the water, partial sun-
light, ground and mobile air, combined
reactively, could have in mind.

Life Comparison

Picked up, a hermit crab who seems
to curl up in a dead snail's shell
from cowardice, attacks the thumb
sustaining him in extraordinary air,
regardless, and if he is attacked
by borers or the other enemies of shells,
he crawls out, raw at the rear!,
to find a new place, thus exposed.
So, he does what is appropriate
within his means, within a case,
and fails: oh he could not bite off
the top whorl of my fingerprint,
although he tried. Therefore, I put
him back to sea for courage, for
his doing what he thinks he has to do
while shrinking, and to propitiate
my own incommensurate enemies,
the firms, establishment, and state.

Cooled Heels Lament Against Frivolity, the Mask of Despair

Dugan's deathward, darling: you
in your unseeable beauty, oh
fictitious, legal person, need
be only formally concerned,
but there is someone too much here,
perspiring in your waiting room.
Because I did not listen when you said,
"Don't call us: we'll call you,"
your credulous receptionist
believes I am a phoney fairy jew
capitalist-commmunist spy
for Antichrist, a deviated mal-
adjusted lobbyist for the Whiskey Trust,
or else accepts me as I am: a fool.
So while I sit here fouling song,
wasting my substance on the air,
the universe is elsewhere, out
the window in the sky. You,
in your inner office, Muse,
smoking a given, good cigar
and swapping dated stories with
star-salesmen of the soul,
refuse to hear my novel pitch
while I sit out here getting old.

On Being Unhappily in Love with Reason

Rage, closest to reason in the mind,
be cold and smile: you can. The smile of rage
is politic and curls with clarity,
though darker than the black hulk of a tooth,
drumming with ache behind a corner of the lips
that smile to ask the apple-cheek of innocence
up Molars' Alley. So, bite. It snaps against
the pit and hard heart of the ripest fruit
and grows a fast tree barked with pain.
Reason, however, chooses, eats, and spits
external forests for its piece of gain.

So, rage will suffer and do harms,
but may it never be extracted from the face
its beast is manned with: lacking rage,
a mouth falls in upon itself in fear,
the furthest from the reason in the mind,
and sucks its own cheek in to chew
blood's living from the fruits of time.
Reason, closest to rage in the mind,
what can you do but loiter in the mean?,
whose golden apples might offend design
but hang there edibly, while civic teeth
gnash at our only air and latest wild,
and keep their fear of reasoning in mind.

Portrait from the Infantry

He smelled bad and was red-eyed with the miseries
of being scared while sleepless when he said
this: "I want a private woman, peace and quiet,
and some green stuff in my pocket. Fuck
the rest." Pity the underwear and socks,
long burnt, of an accomplished murderer,
oh God, of germans and replacements, who
refused three stripes to keep his B.A.R.,
who fought, fought not to fight some days
like any good small businessman of war,
and dug more holes than an outside dog
to modify some Freudian's thesis: "No
man can stand three hundred days
of fear of mutilation and death." What he
theorized was a joke: "To keep a tight
ass-hole, dry socks and a you-deep hole
with you at all times." Afterwards,
met in a sports shirt with a round wife, he was
the clean slave of a daughter, a power brake
and beer. To me, he seemed diminished
in his dream, or else enlarged, who knows?,
by its accomplishment: personal life
wrung from mass issues in a bloody time
and lived out hiddenly. Aside from sound
baseball talk, his only interesting remark
was, in pointing to his wife's belly, "If
he comes out left foot first" (the way
you Forward March!), "I am going to stuff
him back up." "Isn't he awful?" she said.

On an Architect

1

A mine is a hollow tree upside-down in the ground:
the galleries branch out into rooms like leaves
facing and feeding off the rock the way the leaves
exert their palms against the air and drink it.
The tree of earth in the air and its reverse,
the tree of air in the earth, grow up and down
until the word comes: "Put everything back as it was."
Then, after the thundering earthquakes and lightning
of the earth in air, they are no longer there in the same
miraculous silence of their having been there,
except for some hollow and some solid trash
and the metaphysical difference surviving in the image.

2

We poured a pulverized mountain of cement
around an orange-painted mineful of iron
and formed it harder than the term
"concrete" when used in metaphysics to
contrast to "nothing." From the squat
cyclopean basements to the rococo heights
it was a dream. "Fuck 'em all!" I said.
"The janitor can run a jacob's ladder up
the Giants' Staircase and put folding chairs
for hire in the Great Hall: let them pee out
the Rose Window if they have to: there is no
plumbing in my monument." It is; it is
an iron tree, concrete in leaf, meant
to cement man's presence to eternity,
and people pay to enter and be small,
but on these hazy, violet days and with

the sun behind it, oh it seems
almost to disappear, so I went up to it
and hit it. "By my forehead's blood,
oh tricky senses, oh Empirical Philosophers,
I wear the ache that proves it to be there
and not, as light reports, a condensation of the air."

Letter to Donald Fall

I walked a hangover like my death down
the stairs from the shop and opened the door
to a spring snow sticking only to the tops
of air-conditioners and convertibles, and thought
of my friend Donald Fall in San Francisco.
Toothless in spring!, old friend, I count
my other blessings after friendship
unencumbered by communion: I have:
a money-making job, time off it, a wife
I still love sometimes unapproachably
hammering on picture frames, my own
city that I wake to, that the snow
has come to noiselessly at night, it's there
by morning, swallowing the sounds of spring
and traffic, and my new false teeth,
shining and raw in the technician's lab
like Grails, saying, "We are the resurrection
and the life: tear out the green stumps
of your aching and put plastic on instead:
immortality is in science and machines."
I, as an aging phoney, stale, woozy, and corrupt
from unattempted dreams and bad health habits,
am comforted: the skunk cabbage generates its
frost-thawing fart-gas in New Jersey and the first
crocuses appear in Rockefeller Center's Channel Gardens:
Fall, it is not so bad at Dugan's Edge.

Thesis, Antithesis, and Nostalgia

Not even dried-up leaves,
skidding like ice-boats on
their points down winter streets,
can scratch the surface of
a child's summer and its wealth:
a stagnant calm that seemed
as if it must go on and on
outside of cyclical variety
the way, at child-height on a wall,
a brick named "Ann"
by someone's piece of chalk
still loves the one named "Al"
although the street is vacant and
the writer and the named are gone.

Triptych

Scoundrels, Scoundrels

ADAM SMITH

Wheat is probably a better food than oats,

but not than potatoes.

Potatoes, however, are perishable.

KARL MARX

But if we are to demand that the rate of profit, say 14.876934. . , should be exactly equal in every business and every year, down to the hundredth decimal place, on pain of degradation to a fiction, we should be grossly misunderstanding the nature of the rate of profit and of economic laws in general—none of them has any reality except as approximation, tendency, average, but not in *immediate* reality.

This is partly due to the fact that their action is thwarted by the simultaneous action of other laws, but also in part to their own nature as

concepts.

JESUS CHRIST

34. Think not that I am come to send peace on earth. I am not come to send peace, but a sword.

35. For I am come to set a man at variance against his father, and the daughter against her mother and the daughter-in-law against her mother-in-law.

General Prothalamion for Wartimes

Marry. Sweets, tarts and sweets,
come among soots and sherds.
The dairy of the breasts
and warehouse of the balls
will out-last granaries
when grains and futures fall,

granted a lasting. Lust
that lasts a bloodshot night
protected from the air
will breakfast in wrecked day,
excused because it must,
and find its scavenge there.

Given a harvest of wives
and lopping-off of males,
granted that some survive,
the warden of the weak
is number, blood's variety
marauding in the streets.

So, penis, guide the flesh
to shelter in the womb
when sirens and the police
lament all other homes,
and if born, suckling mouths
grow privily with fangs,

well, fangs are promises
to live on what is left,
granted some leavings, and
monsters are replies.
So, marry. Sours and sweets
come among shots and cries.

On the Elk, Unwitnessed

The frantic elk climb from the valleys to escape the flies.
Then, on the heights, they leap, run, and play in snow
as Alces, Alces, glad to be relieved of goads
and ready to get married, due to the wholesome airs.
Those gads downhill, buzzing in armor causative,
must have their joys in cycles too, if the escape
from them in dancing Io!, Io!, on the heights is how,
oh Alces!, Alces!, Hymen triumphs and the roaring stags
fight to assemble harems in the trampled snow
while gad-eggs cradle in their hides and nostrils.

They set out every year diagonally to make
the grand tour of their corner of the world in Oregon,
spurred by a bug at base and climbing up to love
on the apex, and without that lightning touch of Zeus
to slap them, Ha!, Epaphus!, out of the cycling dark
and innocent present of the locally driven beasts,
and toward the widening drive all over Asia and up
into the sky, too, that is the cycle of the really stung.

Grace for Thursday

God help us on a day
like this and one of many.
This day was full
of merciful activity
but we got through
at last to supper: lamb
will be good but do
no good: Christ knows
where it will be
tomorrow down the drain.
Oh it was slaughtered like
himself and hung to dry,
so may we eat it up,
talking in mindless ease,
and by the fish-wife,
Mary, star of the sea,
ride out the night
and eat some fish on Friday.

Stutterer

Courage: your tongue has left
its natural position in the cheek
where eddies of the breath
are navigable calms. Now
it locks against the glottis or
is snapped at by the teeth,
in mid-stream: it must be work
to get out what you mean:
the rapids of the breath
are furious with belief
and want the tongue, as blood
and animal of speech,
to stop it, block it or come clean
over the rocks of teeth
and down the races of the air,
tumbled and bruised to death.
Relax it into acting, be
the air's straw-hat
canoeist with a mandolin
yodeling over the falls.
This is the sound advice
of experts and a true despair:
it is the toll to pass the locks
down to the old mill stream
where lies of love are fair.

Holiday

After hundreds of years of common sense
action appeared at the corners of all eyes:
lights appeared at night, and sounds of war
whammed from the desert back of town.

At first only the outlying saints saw them,
but later they strolled through the streets:
bat-faced devils walking arm in arm
with blond white angels in a tourists' truce.

It was then that Natural Law was repealed
and a public virgin wept that it was she
to whom a fiend or angel had appeared
announcing an unearthly rape of sorts
and the arrival of a difficult child.

On the Supposed Immorality of Orchids

Orchids are poisonous blooms, though
beautiful, because they flower
rootloose on the air and suck,
instead of solid food,
the vicious disposition of the wind.
Paolo!, Francesca!, with no hope
of hold: take heart in air
as sustenance for flight: plants
can root in the uprooting wind
and take, as rationale,
equivocal beauties from thin air.

Trees get choked by their bouquets
but give support. They praise the bloom.
I damn the means.
Praise teaches. In hunting ways
to root in air but succor hosts,
a moral botanist might find
juster symbiotics on the wind:
plants that will pay, for arboring,
a decorative, fair return,
and trees that will survive
the grapples of the flowers.

Memories of Verdun

The men laughed and baaed like sheep
and marched across the flashing day
to the flashing valley. A shaved
pig in a uniform led the way.

I crawled down Old Confusion, hid,
and groaned for years about my crime:
was I the proper coward, they
heroically wrong? I lived out their time!,

a hard labor, convict by look and word:
I was the fool and am penitent:
I was afraid of a nothing, a death;
they were afraid of less, its lieutenant.

Wall, Cave, and Pillar Statements, After Asôka

In order to perfect all readers
the statements should be carved
on rock walls, on cave walls,
and on the sides of pillars so
the charm of their instruction can
affect the mountain climbers near
the cliffs, the plainsmen near
the pillars, and the city people near
the caves they go to on vacations.

The statements should, and in a fair
script, spell out the right text and gloss
of the Philosopher's jocular remark. Text:
"Honesty is the best policy." Gloss:
"He means not 'best' but 'policy,'
(this is the joke of it) whereas in fact
      Honesty is Honesty, Best
      is Best, and Policy is Policy,
      the three terms being not
      related, but here loosely allied.
What is more important is that 'is'
is, but the rock-like truth of the text
resides in the 'the'. The 'the' is The.
      By this means the amusing sage
      has raised or caused to be raised
      the triple standard in stone:
the single is too simple for life,
the double is mere degrading hypocrisy,
but the third combines the first two
in a possible way, and contributes
something unsayable of its own:
this is the pit, nut, seed or stone
of the fruit when the fruit has been
digested: It is good to do good for the wrong

59

reason, better to do good for the good
reason, and best of all to do good
good: i.e.: when the doer and doee
and whatever passes between them
are beyond all words like 'grace'
or 'anagogic insight,' or definitions like
'particular instance of a hoped-at-law,'
and which the rocks alone can convey.
This is the real reason for the rock walls,
the cave walls and pillars, and not the base
desires for permanence and display
that the teacher's conceit suggests."

That is the end of the statements, but,
in order to go on a way after the end
so as to make up for having begun
after the beginning, and thus to come around
to it in order to include the whole thing,
add: "In some places the poignant slogan,
'Morality is a bad joke like everything else'
may be written or not, granted that space
exists for the vulgar remarks, the dates,
initials and hearts of lovers, and all
other graffiti of the prisoners of this world."

THE YALE SERIES OF YOUNGER POETS, which is designed to provide a publishing medium for the first volumes of promising poets, is open to men and women under forty who have not previously had a book of verse published. The Editor of the Series selects the winning volume in the annual contest and writes a preface for it. Manuscripts are received between March 1 and May 1 only; they should be addressed to the Editor, Yale Series of Younger Poets, Yale University Press, New Haven, Connecticut. Rules of the contest will be sent upon request.

31. Worn Earth.   PAUL H. ENGLE
32. Dark Hills Under.   SHIRLEY BARKER
33. Permit Me Voyage.   JAMES AGEE
34. Theory of Flight.   MURIEL RUKEYSER
35. The Deer Come Down.   EDWARD WEISMILLER
36. The Gardener Mind.   MARGARET HALEY
37. Letter to a Comrade.   JOY DAVIDMAN
38. The Connecticut River and Other Poems.
     REUEL DENNEY
39. Return Again, Traveler.   NORMAN ROSTEN
40. The Metaphysical Sword.   JEREMY INGALLS
41. For My People.   MARGARET WALKER
42. Love Letter from an Impossible Land.
     WILLIAM MEREDITH
43. Cut Is the Branch.   CHARLES E. BUTLER
44. Family Circle.   EVE MERRIAM
45. Poems.   JOAN MURRAY
46. A Beginning.   ROBERT HORAN
47. The Grasshopper's Man and Other Poems.
     ROSALIE MOORE
48. A Change of World.   ADRIENNE CECILE RICH
49. A Mask for Janus.   WILLIAM S. MERWIN
50. Various Jangling Keys.   EDGAR BOGARDUS
51. An Armada of Thirty Whales.   DANIEL G. HOFFMAN
52. Some Trees.   JOHN L. ASHBERY
53. The Green Wall.   JAMES WRIGHT
54. A Crackling of Thorns.   JOHN HOLLANDER
55. Of the Festivity.   WILLIAM DICKEY
56. Bone Thoughts.   GEORGE STARBUCK
57. Poems.   ALAN DUGAN
58. Views of Jeopardy.   JACK GILBERT

VOLUMES 48, 52, 54–58 ARE IN PRINT

THE YALE PAPERBOUNDS